£3.95

Written by Tony Lynch Layout and Design by Bill Hill(W.H. Print Design) Photographs supplied by All Action Photographic cover, end papers(inserts), pages 12, 28, 53, 57; All Sport pages 8, 9, 13, 14, 16, 24, 25, 34, 38, 49(top and bottom middle), 50, 51, 52, 55, 56; Syndication International page 11, 15, 18, 19, 22, 26, 27, 31, 33, 36, 37, 40, 41, 42, 43, 60, 61; Associated Sports Photography End papers(main pic) pages 17, 29, 35, 45, 49(bottom left and right), 54, 59; Hulton-Deutsch Collection pages 20, 21, 30, 32; United Sports Picture Agency page 58. Page 7 supplied by John Harris.

Published by

GRANDREAMS LIMITED,
Jadwin House, 205/211 Kentish Town Road,
London NW5 2JU.

Printed in Italy

ISBN 0 86227 677 2

All information contained in this book is correct at time of going to press.

CONTENTS

CHAPTER 1
BEGINNINGS

The Manchester United story begins way back in 1878 when workers at the Newton Heath depot of the Lancashire and Yorkshire Railway decided to form a football team. They simply called themselves Newton Heath (LYR) Football Club and they played in green and gold halved shirts.

The club found a rough, stony ground to play on at North Road, Newton Heath in North-West Manchester. The pitch was situated near a clay pit, and the changing rooms were located in a pub, called The Three Crowns, half-a-mile away!

Newton Heath's earliest games were against other railway teams dotted around Lancashire. At this level they proved virtually unbeatable and easily dominated the competition.

They soon began to look for tougher, more challenging opposition. Opponents in this period included a Bolton Wanderers XI, the Manchester Arcadians and Bootle Reserves.

In 1885 professionalism in football became legal - and so Newton Heath turned professional. In that season they reached the final of the Manchester Cup for the first time, but lost to a team called Hurst. In 1886 they won the trophy.

That year a tough Welshman named Jack Powell joined the club as a full back. He was to become a major influence in the side which also included goalkeeper Tom Hay, and the Doughty brothers - Jack and Roger - signed from Welsh club Druids.

1887 again saw Newton Heath (LYR) in the final of the Manchester Cup - the third of seven consecutive appearances in this final.

Elsewhere in football things were developing fast. 1888 saw the founding of the Football League with twelve top clubs from the North and the Midlands - Accrington Stanley, Aston Villa, Blackburn Rovers, Bolton Wanderers, Burnley, Derby County, Everton, Notts County, Preston North End, Stoke City, West Bromwich Albion and Wolverhampton Wanderers.

Newton Heath (LYR) had ambitions to join the League, but felt they were not quite ready. Instead they joined the Football Alliance in 1889. This was a league formed of twelve clubs *almost* good enough for the Football League. Besides Newton Heath there were the forerunners of many of today's top teams - Birmingham St. Georges, Bootle, Crewe Alexandra, Darwen, Grimsby Town, Long Eaton, Nottingham Forest, Sheffield Wednesday, Small Heath, Sunderland Albion and Walsall Town Swifts.

In their first Alliance season 'The Heathens' (as Newton Heath had become known) finished in 8th position. They also made their first appearance in the FA Cup competition, but were drawn away in the first round against Preston North End who beat them 6-1. In the previous season Preston had achieved a League and Cup 'double' and were known as the 'Invincibles' - so it was no disgrace to lose to them.

In 1890-91 Newton Heath - having dropped the LYR from their name - finished in 9th position and reached the 2nd round of the FA Cup.

The following season 1891-92 saw them in second place behind Nottingham Forest. In the FA Cup that year they had defeated neighbouring Ardwick 5-1. (Ardwick would later become Manchester City.)

The Manchester United team for season1903/4.
Back row: Blackstock, Read, Bacon, Saunders, Bonthron.
Middle row: J. Taylor, Sutcliffe, Downie, Griffiths, Cartwright, Moger, Robertson, Bell, Valentine, J.J. Bower.
Front row: West, McCartney, Pegg, Schofield, Morrison, Stafford, Arkesden, A. Robertson, T. Robertson, Hayes, J.J. Bently.

CHAPTER 2
JOINING THE LEAGUE

Since its inception in 1888 the Football League had expanded to 14 clubs. In 1892 it was decided to establish a First and Second Division. Being Alliance runners-up meant that Newton Heath - together with Alliance Champions Nottingham Forest and 3rd placed Sheffield Wednesday - would automatically gain membership of the First Division for the 1892-93 season. The Second Division was made up of the remainder of the old Alliance.

Newton Heath began League life on 3rd September 1892, away to Blackburn Rovers, who by then had already won the FA Cup five times. In the event an exciting match ended in a 4-3 victory to Rovers. Newton Heath's first Division One team was: Warner, Clements, Brown, Perring, Stewart, Erentz, Farman, Coupar, Donaldson, Carson, Mathieson.

A week later the team made its home League debut at North Road in a 1-1 draw with Burnley.

The Heathens did not win a League match until 15th October 1892 - but they did it in style, beating Wolverhampton Wanderers by a massive 10-1 margin. The score line included hat tricks by Donaldson and Stewart, with the remaining goals coming from Carson, Farman, Hendry and Hood.

Yet, despite this impressive display Newton Heath managed to finish bottom of the First Division in their first season. In those days relegation and promotion were decided by a series of 'test matches' fought out between the bottom three clubs of Division One and the top three in Division Two.

Newton Heath won through to the final test match against Second Division champions, Small Heath (later to become Birmingham City). The game was played at Stoke City's ground and ended in a 1-1 draw. The replay, at Bramall Lane, Sheffield, saw Newton Heath win convincingly by a 5-2 margin. And so they stayed in the top flight.

The club then found a new home, at Bank Street in the Clayton district of Manchester. This ground was little better than North Street had been and was dominated by the belching chimneys of a neighbouring chemical works.

At the end of the 1893-94 season they found themselves once more at the foot of the First Division, having lost 22 of their 30 matches. This time their luck ran out at the test match stage when a 2-0 defeat by Liverpool sent the Heathens into Division Two.

One consequence of the drop was the fact that League rivalry began with Manchester City who, as Ardwick, had been founder members of Division Two. The Heathens first League match against City was played at City's ground in Hyde Road. Newton Heath won 5-2.

In 1896 the club changed its colours to white shirts and blue shorts.

THE RED DEVILS

MARK HUGHES

JIM LEIGHTON

CHAPTER 3

UNITED WE STAND

Believe it or not, a shaggy dog story plays a significant part in the next episode of the club's history!

In 1901, Newton Heath found themselves languishing in the middle of the Second Division. Attendances had fallen, money had been spent on new players and ground improvements - and the club was in dire financial straits.

It was decided to hold a fund raising four-day bazaar at the St. James' Hall in Manchester. Among the attractions was a St. Bernard dog belonging to team captain Harry Stafford. The dog wandered among the crowd with a collecting box around its neck. At one point in the proceedings the dog ran away and was later found by a certain John Davies, a wealthy brewer. Davies tracked Stafford down and bought the dog as a present for his daughter. In the course of their meeting Davies learned of the financial plight of the Newton Heath club.

In the winter of 1902 it looked as if the club could no longer continue when its creditors began to call in their debts. At this point Davies and three other businessmen stepped in with the necessary funds. In return Davies became chairman and his partners took a controlling interest in the club.

On 28th April, 1902 it was decided to re-name the club. A number of suggestions were put forward, including 'Manchester Central' and 'Manchester Celtic'. But it was Louis Rocca - later to become a famous scout for the club - who first suggested 'Manchester United'. It was a name destined to become the most famous in football.

At the same time the club changed its colours once more - to red shirts and white shorts.

In its first season under the Manchester United banner (1902-03), the team finished a respectable fifth in Division Two (neighbouring Manchester City were promoted that year).

In September 1903 the club's secretary, James West, resigned. His replacement was Earnest Mangnall, formerly secretary of Burnley FC. Mangnall was to become the first truly effective driving force behind Manchester United. In his first season the club finished third in Division Two, a position they managed to repeat in 1904-05.

Then, in 1905-06 Manchester United were Division Two runners-up, to Bristol City, and so earned promotion back to the top flight. (The system of promoting the top two clubs in Division Two and relegating the two at the foot of the First, had been adopted by the League in 1898). In 1907-08 Manchester United became League Champions for the first time.

Mangnall had built a splendid squad of players, including the Welsh wizard, Billy Meredith - signed from Manchester City for £500 - Harold Halse, Alex 'Sandy' Turnbull, James Turnbull, Herbert Burgess, Jimmy Banister and captain Charlie Roberts.

In 1908 they became the first ever winners of the FA Charity Shield, beating QPR 4-0 after a 1-1 draw. In 1909 they reached their first FA Cup Final, against Bristol City at the Crystal Palace in London. 67,651 fans turned out, many Mancunians making the long journey south to see United's 1-0 victory with a goal from Sandy Turnbull.

On the way to the final United had beaten Blackburn Rovers by a resounding 6-1 margin, in the third round. In the 4th, against Burnley in snowbound conditions, they had been losing 0-1 when the game was abandoned 18 minutes from the final whistle. United won the replay 3-2. In the semi-final they had beaten Newcastle United, the eventual League Champions.

After the final United returned to Manchester and were treated like conquering heroes. They arrived at the Central Station to be greeted by crowds of cheering fans. Earnest Mangnall proudly carried the English Cup, and many of his players were hoisted shoulder high before reaching the carriages which would take them through the streets of the city to the Town Hall in Albert Square.

THE RED DEVILS PROFILE

BILLY MEREDITH

Billy Meredith was the first of the great Manchester United legends - and a great character, too. He was a right winger of outstanding talent who played with a toothpick in his mouth and would often chat with spectators when the ball was on the other side of the pitch!

Meredith was born in Chirk, North Wales, and began his footballing career with a local side before playing for Northwich Victoria. In 1894 he was signed as an amateur by Manchester City where his talents truly blossomed. In the 1904 FA Cup Final he scored the winning goal for City against Bolton Wanderers.

He joined Manchester United in a £500 deal in 1906 and soon proved his worth, winning a Cup Winners' medal in 1909 and League Championship medals in 1907-08 and 1910-11.

Billy Meredith was capped 48 times by Wales. He returned to Manchester City in 1921 to finish off a remarkable career spanning 29 years and almost 700 games. He died in 1958.

THE RED DEVILS

MAL DONAGHY

THE
RED DEVILS
BRIAN McCLAIR

CHAPTER 4

OLD TRAFFORD

So pleased was Chairman John Davies with United's cup success that he gave the then phenomenal sum of £60,000 for the purchase and building of a new stadium. This was to be Old Trafford, on the Manchester/Salford border, now one of the most famous footballing venues in the world.

And so United played their last game at Bank Street on 22nd January, 1910, where a mere 7000 fans turned out to watch them beat Spurs 5-0.

Manchester United's first game at their magnificent new stadium was played against Liverpool. This time more than 45,000 turned up for the game and saw United lose 3-4 after being 2-0 and then 3-1 up! That season they finished fifth in Division One.

In 1910-11 United hit the heights again by pipping Aston Villa to the post by a single point in the race for the Championship.

In 1912, Earnest Mangnall left Old Trafford to become manager of Manchester City. It was the end of a Golden Era for United - they would not win another League Championship for more than 40 years.

Old Trafford is one of Britain's finest football stadiums and a favourite for many fans and players. On a match day the ground is a seething cauldron of red and white excitement and atmosphere. However well (or poorly!) United are faring, Old Trafford is consistently among the best attended grounds in the country. Record attendance is 76,962 for the FA Cup semi-final between Grimsby and Wolves in March 1939. The record for a League match is 70,504 when United played Aston Villa on Boxing Day, 1920. Today the ground's capacity is set at 56,385.

Before the start of the 1909-10 season, a number of Manchester United players rebelled against the League and the FA on behalf of the Union of Professional Footballers, a body which was finding official recognition hard to come by. Just 24 hours before the start of the season the authorities relented and the Union was recognised. During the dispute the United team became known as 'The Outcasts'.

CHAPTER 5
THE BARREN YEARS

Between 1911and 1939 Manchester United, while still considered a glamour team and a big draw wherever they played, could not achieve the League success they and their fans so desperately wanted.

They finished in 4th place in 1912-13, but after that came a gradual decline which saw them consistently in the lower half of the table, until in 1921-22 they finished in 22nd position and plunged into Division Two.

United fought the 1922-23 campaign valiantly hoping for a swift return to the top flight. But two late defeats by Blackpool and Leicester City put paid to that ambition.

1923-34 was an indifferent season for the club and they finished 14th in the Second Division.

Then in 1924-25 came a fine revival. United played consistently well throughout the season - losing only one home game, against Oldham Athletic - to finish as runners-up to Leicester City and gain promotion back to the First Division.

In their return season (1925-26), United finished 9th, 13 points behind Champions Huddersfield, the team which the great Herbert Chapman had made into the toast of the twenties.

But Manchester United were to stay in Division One for just six seasons before sinking again in 1930-31 with a mere 22 points.

By then Old Trafford was engulfed in financial worries, no thanks to some unwise speculation in the transfer market. Midway through the 1931-32 season, United came to a crisis point in their history. The club faced bankruptcy - indeed funds were so low that when the players went to collect their wages during Christmas week, they discovered there was no money with which to pay them!

But rescue was at hand in the shape of a local clothing manufacturer, James W. Gibson. Gibson loved football and agreed to help the club. He invested a staggering £22,000 of his own money to pay off the debts and meet the players' wages. He was then voted onto the Manchester United board and within a short while became club Chairman.

United needed a similar miracle on the field!

A new manager, A. Scott Duncan, was appointed in July 1932. But United managed only 6th position that season and were resigned to staying in Division Two.

1933-34 saw them finish in 20th place, and at their lowest ebb since joining the Football League. In fact Manchester United only just avoided the drop into the Third Division (North) by winning the last match of the season 2-0 against Millwall.

The close proximity of the Third Division put a scare into the Red Devils. New players were drafted in for the next season and they managed 5th position. Then, in 1935-36 United won the Second Division title, four points ahead of Charlton Athletic.

But these were the yo-yo years for United. No sooner had they arrived back in Division One than they were relegated again, along with Sheffield Wednesday.

The next season (1937-38) saw them bounce right back as Second Division runners-up to Aston Villa. It had been a close fought campaign and was only decided on United's superior goal average over Sheffield United. Nevertheless, it was enough to put the club back where it belonged and was to prove yet another turning point in the history of Manchester United.

There was, however, to be an interruption in the proceedings. United were just getting back into their stride - finishing 14th in Division One in 1938-39 - when World War II began and football was suspended for the duration.

Jack Rowley - in his day one of the most dangerous shots in soccer.

CLAYTON
BLACKMORE

NORMAN WHITESIDE

CHAPTER 6
ENTER MATT BUSBY

On 15th February, 1945, the board of Manchester United appointed as their new manager an ex-Scottish international half-back who had enjoyed a fine playing career with Manchester City and Liverpool. His name was Matt Busby and he was destined to lead United to glory - although that road would be paved with tragedy.

Busby's task was to be a tough one. When he took over as manager he inherited a club with a £15,000 overdraft at the bank - and no ground to play on!

Old Trafford had suffered perhaps more than any other football stadium in German bombing raids during the war. The main stand, offices and dressing rooms had all been destroyed and there was even a small tree sprouting up through the debris!

When Chairman James Gibson offered Matt Busby a three year contract, Busby insisted on five years - to give himself enough time to build an effective squad. Busby also took on Jimmy Murphy, an ex-Welsh international and West Bromwich Albion wing-half, as United's chief coach.

At that time United's books included several fine players: Johnny Carey - an Irish international and team

captain; Jack Rowley - a no-nonsense goal-getting centre-forward; Johnny Morrison an ultra-intelligent inside forward; Allenby Chilton - a powerful centre-half; Stan Pearson - a sharp-shooting inside-left; Charlie Mitton - a speedy left winger; John Aston - Carey's partner at full- back; and goalkeeper Jack Crompton. Busby's first venture into the transfer market proved to be a shrewd one when he signed experienced winger Jimmy Delaney from Celtic for £5,000. These players were the nucleus of Matt Busby's first great United team.

In 1946-47, the first official season after the war, they finished as First Division runners-up, just one point behind Liverpool. United repeated the feat in the following season - but went on to even greater glory by winning the FA Cup for the second time.

United's cup trail had begun in the Third Round at Villa Park, where within 30 seconds they had found themselves a goal down. This fired them into action and by half-time they had come back with a vengeance to lead by a 5-1 margin. The final score in this remarkable cup-tie was Aston Villa 4, Manchester United 6.

Liverpool were the 4th Round victims - 3-0, then came Charlton - 2-0 and Preston - 4-1. The semi-final, played at Hillsborough, saw United up against 1946 Cup winners Derby County. A hat trick by Stan Pearson put paid to

Page 18 top: *Matt Busby in his Manchester City playing days.* Below: *Receiving the Freedom of the City from Manchester's Lord Major in 1967.*
Page 19 left: *Jimmy Delaney,* right: *Jack Rowley,* below: *Jack Crompton.*

HIS FIRST TRIUMPH

ENTER MATT BUSBY

Derby's hopes.

Remarkably, all of United's opponents en route to the final had been from the First Division.

Manchester United's opponents in the 1948 FA Cup Final were Blackpool, a team which included the legendary English internationals Stanley Matthews and Stan Mortensen. The game has gone down in history as one of the Great Finals.

With just 20 minutes remaining Blackpool led 2-1. Then came an astonishing comeback by United with goals from Rowley, Pearson and Anderson to snatch the trophy from the *Seasiders'* grasp. In winning the match, United became the first club to win the cup after having twice been behind.

After finishing as League runners-up again in 1948-49 and in 1950-51, United finally won the Championship, for the third time, in 1951-52. Jack Rowley was the leading scorer that season with 30 goals, including two hat tricks in the first two games of 1951. Closest rivals were the North London duo of Spurs and Arsenal who both finished on 53 points, behind United's 57.

In the last game of that memorable season United crowned their glory with a magnificent 6-1 drubbing of Arsenal, with goals from Rowley (3), Pearson (2) and Byrne. It was Manchester United's first Championship for 41 years.

All pictures from the 1948 FA Cup Final, Manchester United v Blackpool. Bottom: *Jack Crompton, United's 'keeper, thwarts Blackpool's Stan Mortensen.* Middle: *Rowley heads powerfully for goal.* Top: *Rowley, on ground, scores United's second goal.*

THE RED DEVILS PROFILE

JOHNNY CAREY

Johnny Carey was United's first post-war captain. He led the team to its FA Cup triumph of 1948 and the League Championship of 1951-52. He was an inspirational right back, but was also able to play in virtually any position on the field - indeed he once played in goal!

Carey was born in Dublin and played international football for both the Republic of Ireland and Northern Ireland. He also captained the Rest of Europe team against England in 1947. He was voted Footballer of the Year in 1949.

CHAPTER 7
THE BUSBY BABES

Knowing that all great teams eventually disintegrate, Matt Busby was determined that continuity and consistency would be the rule at Old Trafford. And so, while United's first great post-war team had been marching to glory under his inspired leadership, the foundations of another wave of great players were being laid via the club's youth development policy.

To keep the club supplied with potential players a network of scouts was built up all over the British Isles - and the players selected became known as 'The Busby Babes'. The most successful 'Babes' were groomed and cultivated by United's experienced coaching staff, under the watchful eye of Jimmy Murphy, and gradually each one made his way through the ranks from the youth team to the reserves.

United found the League tough going in 1952-53, and Busby began to draft some of the youngsters into the first team.

During that season, names soon to become familiar wherever football was played, began to appear in United's programmes - among them were Jackie Blanchflower, John Doherty, David Pegg, Dennis Viollet, Jeff Whitefoot and Duncan Edwards. Busby supplemented his young team with the talents of Tommy Taylor, a quicksilver centre forward signed from Blackpool for £29,999 (an odd figure, but Busby did

not want Taylor tagged with a £30,000 price on his head).

United finished 8th in 1952-53 - and Busby decided it was now time to bring his 'Babes' to the forefront.

The next two seasons were to prove an effective settling in period for the new look team. In 1953-54 they finished in 4th position and in 1954-55 they were 5th. They were also drawing huge crowds at every match as football fans everywhere sensed that Manchester United were once again a very special team.

In 1955-56 the ' Manchester Magic' worked beyond all expectations. That season saw United winning the League Championship by an amazing 11 point margin from nearest rivals Blackpool and Wolves.

In '56-57 United went one better. They won the League Championship *and* reached the final of the FA Cup, against Aston Villa. They now looked certain to become the first team since Villa, in 1897, to win the coveted League and Cup 'double'.

But football is a fickle game - and things were not to go United's way at Wembley.

Only six minutes of the game had passed when Ray Woods in the United goal was charged by Villa winger Peter McParland. Both players fell to the ground and Woods had to be carried off with a broken cheekbone. These were the days before substitutes were allowed - so Jackie Blanchflower took over in goal.

Although they battled valiantly, United eventually lost 1-2, and the dream of the 'double' was shattered.

The Manchester United team of 1958. Back row: *Tom Curry(trainer), Duncan Edwards, Mark Jones, Ray Wood, Bobby Charlton, Bill Foulkes, Matt Busby (manager).* Front row: *John Berry, Bill Whelan, Roger Byrne, David Pegg, Eddie Colman.*

THE RED DEVILS

PAUL McGRATH

THE
RED DEVILS
STEVE BRUCE
SHARP

CHAPTER 8

INTO EUROPE

Matt Busby dreamed of seeing Manchester United playing alongside the best teams in Europe - and following the successful Championship campaign of 1955-56 United became the first English club to enter the European Cup competition.

In the preliminary round they took on Belgian champions Anderlect, and won by a resounding 12-0 aggregate over two legs. Then came aggregate victories over Borussia Dortmund and Athletico Bilbao to place United in the semi-finals, against Real Madrid - Europe's dominant team of the period and the first holders of the European Cup. In the event, Real won 5-3 on aggregate - but United's fine performance in the competition had whetted the English appetite for European success.

Winning the League Championship in 1956-57 meant that United would have a second chance at European glory in the '57-58 season.

They began that campaign with high hopes, but were to end it in tragedy.

The first tie, in the preliminary round, was against Irish Champions Shamrock Rovers - United won 9-2 on aggregate. Dukla Prague, of Czechoslovakia, were the next victims - a 3-1 aggregate victory for United.

This took them to the quarter-finals where they were drawn against Red Star Belgrade, the Champions of Yugoslavia. The first leg was played on 14th January 1958, at Old Trafford. United's team: Gregg, Foulkes, Byrne, Colman, Jones, Edwards, Morgans, Charlton, Taylor (T), Viollet and Scanlon - won 2-1, with goals from Eddie Colman and Bobby Charlton.

At that time the Busby Babes were undoubtedly the most exciting team in British football, drawing massive crowds wherever they played.

On 1st February the team travelled to Highbury to play Arsenal in the League. Ten minutes into the game United took the lead through the powerful Duncan Edwards. Twenty minutes later they were two-up with an end-to-end goal finished off magnificently by the young Bobby Charlton. Just before half-time centre-forward Tommy Taylor made it 3-0 with a precision goal that left the Gunners' defence floundering. The game looked to be well and truly sewn up by the Babes. But then came the second half - and a string of the kind of surprises that make soccer such a superb game to watch.

The score remained 3-0 to United until, with half-an-hour left to play, Arsenal drew level within the space of three minutes with goals by Herd and Bloomfield (2).

Any run-of-the-mill team could have been forgiven for settling for a draw - but Manchester United were special.

Dennis Viollet

They fought back from the point of crisis to once again dominate the proceedings. A flowing move between Charlton and Scanlon found inside-forward Dennis Viollet ready and willing to head the ball past Arsenal's 'keeper Jack Kelsey, to regain the lead. United's fifth came from Tommy Taylor, squeezing the ball into the net from an almost impossible angle. Arsenal scored again through Tapscott - but United were the deserving winners at 5-4.

That match has gone down in the annuls of Football League history as one of the finest ever played. It also has a sad significance - as an epitaph for a truly great team. For within a week Manchester United would be destroyed.

Of all the talented Busby Babes, Duncan Edwards was perhaps the shining star. He was born in Dudley, Worcestershire, in 1936. As an 11 year-old he was considered good enough to play for Dudley Boys', alongside players three years his senior. He was snapped up by Manchester United in 1952 and made his first team debut - in the No.6 shirt - on 4th April, 1953, in a 1-4 defeat by Cardiff City.

Over the next four seasons Duncan Edwards went on to make 175 appearances for Manchester United, mainly at left-half, occasionally at inside-forward. He was an immensely talented and physically commanding player, combining a true footballing brain with a devastating shot in both feet.

In 1955, at just 18 years and 183 days, Edwards became England's youngest ever full international when he was selected to play against Scotland. He went on to win 18 caps.

By 1957 he had won two League Championship medals (1955-56 & 1956-57) and an FA Cup runners-up medal in the 1957 final against Aston Villa.

Sadly we can only guess at the heights Duncan Edwards might have achieved, had his life not been so tragically cut short by the Munich air disaster of 1958. He died from injuries two weeks after the crash.

THE RED DEVILS PROFILE

DUNCAN EDWARDS

THE RED DEVILS

VIV ANDERSON

THE
RED DEVILS
MIKE DUXBURY
SHARP

CHAPTER 9
MUNICH

On 5th February, 1958 Manchester United played their European Cup quarter-final second leg against Red Star in Belgrade, the capital of Yugoslavia. This exciting match - which at one stage saw United 3-0 up, with goals from Viollet and Charlton (2) - ended in a 3-3 draw. But this was enough to give United a 5-4 aggregate win and a place in the semi-finals.

After the game the United players and staff were treated to a warm-hearted banquet given by the Red Star club.

On Thursday 6th February the United party boarded the plane which would take them home. Also on board were eleven British football journalists and six other passengers together with two stewardesses, a steward and the flight deck staff led by Captain James Thain.

The aircraft, a BEA Elizabethan charter plane, with co-pilot Captain Kenneth Rayment at the controls, landed at Munich airport for re-fuelling.

On the journey across South-Eastern Europe the United players had relaxed by playing cards, reading and chatting about that weekend's tough League fixture against Wolves. Now, despite the chill of snowbound Munich there was a warm glow in their hearts as they walked, shivering, to the airport terminal for hot coffee.

They were totally unaware that disaster was to strike them within an hour - a disaster that would shake the world.

By 2pm the aircraft was re-fuelled and the passengers began to board once more. The first attempted take-off was abandoned by Captain Thain because of 'boost surging', a condition which caused the plane's engines to over-accelerate. A second attempt was also abandoned, and the passengers were told to return once again to the terminal lounge.

By then snow had begun to fall quite heavily and several passengers felt it unlikely that the plane would actually take-off again that day. Duncan Edwards even sent a telegram to his landlady in Manchester - it read:

'ALL FLIGHTS CANCELLED FLYING HOME TOMORROW - DUNCAN'.

However, a third take-off attempt was made at 3.03pm on that fateful day.

Again the Elizabethan failed to reach the required speed for take-off. But this time it was too late. "Christ, we won't make it," shouted Captain Rayment.

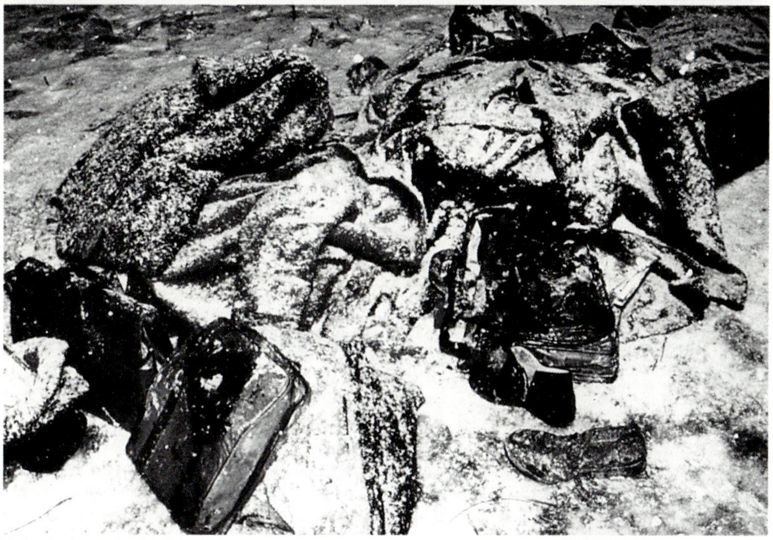

Opposite page: *The ill-fated Manchester United team line-up before the start of their match against Red Star Belgrade.* This page top: *The bodies of the United players arrive back at Manchester Airport.* Right and below: *Some of the wreckage of the crashed aircraft.*

The aircraft careered through the airport perimeter fence, crossed a road and then crashed into a house. This caused the plane to break up. The cockpit hit a tree and the fuselage crashed into a wooden hut which housed a truck loaded with fuel. The truck exploded.

Twenty-three people were to die as a result of the crash. Eight of them were Manchester United players: Roger Byrne, Geoff Bent, Eddie Coleman, Mark Jones, Duncan Edwards, Liam Whelan, Tommy Taylor and David Pegg. Three United officials also perished, as did eight journalists, two aircrew and two other passengers.

Among the injured players were Bobby Charlton, Bill Foulkes, Harry Gregg, Jackie Blanchflower, Dennis Viollet, Albert Scanlon, Ray Woods, Ken Morgans and Johnny Berry. Matt Busby was seriously injured too. For several weeks he was to lay close to death in a Munich hospital.

When news of the crash reached Britain, people were shocked and stunned into disbelief and horrified that a great football team could be destroyed within a matter of minutes. The whole of football mourned the loss.

Back at Old Trafford Jimmy Murphy - Matt Busby's assistant - took over United's managerial duties. (Murphy had not been on the trip to Belgrade because of international duty with the Welsh team).

The next scheduled game against League leaders Wolves was postponed as Murphy attempted a rapid rebuilding programme.

He signed forward Ernie Taylor from Blackpool and drafted him into the team which played in United's first post-Munich match - a fifth round FA Cup-tie against Sheffield Wednesday, at Old Trafford on 19th February, just thirteen days after the disaster at Munich. The game was an emotional one for the players and fans of both teams.

Jimmy Murphy had performed miracles in organising a United squad - apart from Ernie Taylor at inside right, he had also brought forward a number of youngsters from the ranks, including Ian Greaves at left back, Freddy Goodwin at right half, Ronnie Cope at centre half, Colin Webster at outside right, Alex Dawson at centre forward, Mark Pearson at inside left and Shay Brennan on the left-wing.

This squad, comprised mainly of eager youngsters, was surprisingly supplemented at left half by Stan Crowther who, less than twelve months earlier, had played for Aston Villa against Manchester United in the 1957 FA Cup Final. Murphy had persuaded Crowther to sign for United only an hour before the kick-off! Most remarkable of all, however, was the appearance of two players who had survived the air crash and were now match fit again - goalkeeper Harry

Gregg and right-back Bill Foulkes.

59,848 fans turned out to watch the game and make Old Trafford into a virtual cauldron of emotion. In the event, Manchester United played their hearts out to win 3-0 with goals by Shay Brennan (2) and Alex Dawson.

That season United finished 9th in Division One, having inevitably fallen behind in the wake of Munich.

In the FA Cup, however, they rode the waves of emotion and reached Wembley for the second year in succession. Their opponents were Bolton Wanderers, on 3rd May. By then two more survivors of the Munich air crash, Bobby Charlton and Dennis Viollet, were fit again. And on the Wembley touchline, aided by walking sticks, sat Matt Busby.

But this was not to be United's day - Bolton's centre-forward Nat Lofthouse saw to that by first scoring the opening goal with a low drive past Gregg, within five minutes of the kick-off.

Later, during a Bolton attack, Gregg was unable to parry a fierce shot from Dennis Stevens. As United's 'keeper leapt to recapture the ball, Lofthouse charged in and barged him and the ball over the goal-line. Much to everyone's amazement - including Lofthouse's - the referee awarded a goal, in what proved to be one of Wembley's most controversial moments.

The score remained - Bolton Wanderers 2, Manchester United 0 - and United became the first team to lose in consecutive seasons in an FA Cup Final at Wembley.

Five days later United resumed their European Cup challenge in the semi-final against Italian champions AC Milan. United won 2-1 at home, but lost the second leg 0-4.

And so closed Manchester United's most dramatic and tragic season.

Several years later the colour black was incorporated into the official team strip as a mark of respect for those who lost their lives in the snow at Munich.

Opposite page: *The Manchester United squad immediately after Munich.* Above: *Harry Gregg (Manchester United) is treated after his collison with Bolton's Nat Lofthouse during the 1958 FA Cup Final.* Below: *Lofthouse scores Bolton's first goal in the same match.*

Wearing the red No.10 shirt in the 1957 FA Cup Final was a fair-haired youngster named Bobby Charlton, a player destined to become arguably Manchester United's greatest hero.

He was born in Ashington, Northumberland, in 1935, the younger brother of Jack Charlton and a nephew to the great Newcastle United hero, Jackie Milburn.

The young Bobby Charlton was first spotted by United scout Joe Armstrong in 1953. He played for England as a schoolboy and on leaving school decided to join United, despite the interest of several other top clubs. It was an association that would become a soccer legend - all over the world the name of Bobby Charlton is synonymous with that of Manchester United.

Charlton made his League debut on 6th October 1956, scoring two goals against Charlton Athletic. By 1958, having survived the Munich air crash, he was a first team regular and appeared in that season's FA Cup Final against Bolton Wanderers.

Charlton made his full international debut for England in 1958, against Scotland. This was to be the first of 106 caps collected in an international career highlighted by a World Cup winners' medal in 1966. That season he was voted both English Footballer of the Year and European Footballer of the Year.

Bobby Charlton's greatest moment with United was the winning of the European Cup in 1968, against Benfica. He also collected an FA Cup winners medal in 1963 and League Championship medals in 1956-57, 1964-65 and 1966-67.

In 1969 Charlton was awarded the OBE. He played his last game for United against Chelsea at Stamford Bridge in 1974. After that he became manager of Preston, but later turned to the coaching of young footballers with his famous soccer schools. He is now a director of Manchester United Football Club.

THE RED DEVILS PROFILE

BOBBY CHARLTON

CHAPTER 10
REBUILDING

Top: *The victorious Manchester United players show off the FA Cup after their 3-1 triumph over Leicester City in 1963.*
Below: *Pat Crerand, a shrewd buy from Celtic.*

Matt Busby returned to the manager's chair in time for the 1958-59 season. And although his rebuilding task was a mammoth one, he did not rush headlong into the transfer market, as might be expected. Instead, he relied on the tried and trusted youth policy which had produced the backbone of his original Babes.

Suddenly a number of former reserve team players found themselves playing regularly in the first team alongside Munich survivors Charlton, Viollet, Gregg, Foulkes and Scanlon.

Warren Bradley, an amateur international winger, was signed from Bishop Auckland.

It wasn't until a quarter of the way through the season that Busby speculated with a then record transfer fee of £45,000 for Albert Quixall, a centre-forward from Sheffield Wednesday.

Manchester United finished the 1958-59 season as runners-up to Wolves in the League - a remarkable achievement considering the traumas that the club had so recently experienced.

For the next two seasons United finished 7th. Then in 1961-62 they

slumped to 15th position - and Busby had a problem.

This time he did find a solution by wise investments in the transfer market. He had already bought goal ace David Herd from Arsenal for £32,000. Then came arguably the best buy of Matt Busby's managerial career - Denis Law.

Law was then a young Scottish superstar playing for Torino in the Italian League. Busby brought him back to Britain and United for a record £115,000.

Another shrewd Busby signing was that of Pat Crerand for £43,000 from Celtic in February 1963.

That season (1962-63) United finished in 19th position, just above the relegation zone - but they also reached their fifth FA Cup Final, against Leicester City.

The 1963 Cup Final was a game to remember. Man-of-the-Match was undoubtedly the fabulous Law who scored a spectacular opening goal in the 29th minute. David Herd added a second after 58 minutes. Keyworth replied for Leicester later in the game, but Herd sealed the matter with his second goal. United had won 3-1 and it proved to be yet another turning point in the history of the club.

Top: *David Herd showing the scoring form that made him a £32,000 buy from Arsenal.*
Below: *Denis Law, undoubtedly Busby's best-ever buy, is thwarted by Leicester's Gordon Banks in the 1963 Cup Final.*

THE RED DEVILS PROFILE

DENIS LAW

Inside-forward Denis Law would appear in anyone's top ten of players of recent history. He was born in 1940 in Aberdeen. The talented youngster was first spotted by Bill Shankly who was then the manager of Huddersfield Town. 'Shanks' signed the awkward, gawky, spectacle-wearing youth, because he knew that he was a star in the making.

And of course Shankly was right. In 1958 Law became Scotland's youngest-ever full international at 18 years, 236 days, in a match against Wales. Scotland's manager that day was Matt Busby.

After just 80 games with Huddersfield, Law was transferred to Manchester City for £56,000. He stayed at Maine Road for just one season before moving on to Torino, of Italy, in a £110,000 deal. Like a number of other British footballers, Law found his Italian experience an unhappy one. And twelve months later he was snapped up by Busby at United for £115,000.

That was the beginning of a beautiful friendship, for Denis Law went on to become one of Old Trafford's all-time greats. He was a terrific player, full of talent and with lightning fast reflexes. But it was his goal scoring genius that he is best remembered. He scored no less than 236 times in 396 appearances for United.

Law won an FA Cup winners medal in 1963 and League Championship medals in 1965 and 1967. He was voted Footballer of the Year in 1964. He was capped 55 times by Scotland.

In 1973 Law rejoined Manchester City and ironically it was his goal for City which set the seal on United's relegation to Division Two in 1974. Denis now enjoys life as a radio commentator.

CHAPTER 11
THE GREAT YEARS

Manchester United began the 1963-64 season determined to put up a better showing in the League than they had done in the previous season. In the event they finished as runners-up to Liverpool and also reached the FA Cup semi-finals where they lost to West Ham.

Denis Law scored no less than 30 League goals in 30 appearances, Bobby Charlton played in all but two League games - and two youngsters were making their presence felt at Old Trafford. One of them was Nobby Stiles who would later play for England's World Cup winning team. The other was a slightly built lad from Belfast. His name was George Best and he was destined to become one of the most famous footballers of all time.

1964-65 was to be a super season for United. With the addition of winger John Connelly - signed for £60,000 from Burnley - they became the most effective team in the League and won the title on goal average above Leeds United.

The Championship (United's sixth) meant of course that Matt Busby would have another opportunity for European Cup success.

With aggregate victories over HJK Helsinki (9-2) and ASK Vorwaerts (5-1) they reached the quarter-finals against Portugese champions Benfica. United won the first leg, at home, by a 3-2 margin. Then the team travelled to Lisbon for the return match. It was a tough proposition to expect victory against such a strong side on their own territory.

But this was to be a night of inspired football from United - with an extra touch of magic provided by George Best.

After just six minutes Best headed a Tony Dunne free kick into the back of the Benfica net. In the twelfth minute he scored a solo goal of breathtaking brilliance, beating three men en route. Then Best slipped a great pass to John Connelly who converted it into United's third goal. Shay Brennan then scored an unfortunate own goal, but Benfica could not capitalise on the error. Crerand and Charlton saw to that by scoring United's fourth and fifth. Final score: 5-1 to United, they had won the tie 8-3 on aggregate.

Unfortunately the euphoria was to end in the semi-final when United lost by a 2-1 aggregate margin to FK Partizan Belgrade. Matt Busby still had to wait.

1966-67 saw a few new faces in Manchester United's line-up. Bobby Noble (left-back) and Johnny Aston (left-wing) had graduated to the first team through the ranks of the youth squad and the reserves. David Sadler also made a name for himself as a goal-minded midfielder. However, the most effective newcomer was Alex Stepney, bought from Chelsea for £55,000. His sturdy, if unspectacular performances in goal were to prove a major factor in United's superb defence.

The team chalked up some convincing victories in that League campaign - 5-0 against Sunderland, four of the goals coming from David

This page: *Denis Law scores for United in an early European campaign.* Opposite top: *Manchester United's semi-final first leg against Real Madrid in the 1968 European Cup. Best scores the only goal of the game.* Below: *The return leg in Madrid and Brain Kidd turns away after Bill Foulkes scores the goal that clinched the tie.*

Sadler, 4-0 against Blackpool, 5-2 against Leicester City, and the title clincher in May, 6-1 away to West Ham. United won the 1966-67 League Championship four points ahead of Nottingham Forest.

Once again they would have a crack at the European Cup.

They opened the campaign against Hibernian,of Malta - a 4-0 home win and a dour 0-0 away draw took them through to round two where they met FK Sarajevo, of Yugoslavia.

This proved a tough, physical tie with Best, Kidd and Burns on the receiving end of some rather questionable tactics in the away leg: result 0-0. The return at Old Trafford was equally uncompromising - with Sarajevo's skipper being sent off for a wild tackle on Best. Goals from Aston and Best took United through 2-1.

Quarter-final opponents were Gornik Zabrze, of Poland, the team which had already disposed of Dinamo Kiev and Celtic. The first leg, at home, saw United emerge as 2-0 winners with Best once more playing a major role. The second leg was played in bitterly cold and snowy conditions in Gornik. The Poles won 1-0, but that was not enough to prevent United going through 2-1 on aggregate.

So, for the second time in two years Matt Busby's Manchester United found themselves in the semi-final of the European Cup. Real Madrid were the illustrious opponents, promising to make it the glamour match of the tournament. However, the opening game, at Old Trafford, turned out to be a dour one with United finding it almost impossible to penetrate the Spanish defence. The final whistle left the score line at 1-0 to United, thanks to a goal from George Best. It seemed highly unlikely that such a slim lead would be enough to carry them through in Madrid. United still had it all to do.

On 15th May, 1968 the Bernabeu Stadium - home of Real Madrid - was a seething mass of excitement, packed to the rafters with 125,000 fanatical supporters all hoping to see some fabulous football. And the game lived up to all expectations - even if it did disappoint the Spaniards!

United were somewhat weakened by the absence of Denis Law who was unfit. The reshuffled team now included the veteran full back Bill Foulkes - and no one really gave *The Reds* a chance.

By half-time Real were leading 3-1 and it seemed as if United's dreams of reaching the final were to be dashed yet again. But a Busby pep talk during the interval seemed to work wonders. He simply told his players to "Go out there and enjoy yourselves...go out and attack". They proved to be the right words at the right time - United were a changed team in the second half.

The first breakthrough came 15 minutes from the end when Bill Foulkes headed into the Real penalty area. The half chance was snapped up by David Sadler - and the aggregate scores were level.

In the dying minutes of the game Paddy Crerand took a throw-in to Best. Best jinked his way past a string of defenders and passed the ball to big Bill Foulkes who had made a long run from defence. Foulkes calmly side-footed the ball into the net to become the unlikely hero of the hour. United had won.

EUROPEAN CUP FINAL
THE GREAT YEARS

The 1968 European Cup Final between Benfica and Manchester United, was played at Wembley Stadium on 29 May. 100,000 fans turned out that evening to see if the famous '*Red Devils*' could become the first English club to win the trophy. (Ironically, because of a colour clash, United were forced to play the most important match in their history in an all blue strip).

Once again the team was without Denis Law who was in hospital recovering from a cartilege operation. United's line-up read: Stepney, Brennan, Dunne, Crerand, Foulkes, Stiles, Best, Kidd, Charlton (captain), Sadler, Aston.

Compared with what was to come, the first half was a dull affair, keeping the match at stalemate. The second half was more exciting. Bobby Charlton scored the first goal of the match with a header from a Tony Dunne cross. Then David Sadler had the chance to sew it all up for United, but he missed an open goal. Ten minutes from the final whistle Graca cracked in an equaliser for Benfica. The Portugese team almost stole the game when Eusebio broke through, but Stepney saved the day. And so, after 90 minutes the score remained at 1-1.

As the United players sprawled exhausted and drained on the pitch during the break before extra time, Matt Busby rallied them with a characteristically buoyant team talk, combining tactics with encouragement.

The first seven minutes of extra time were as exciting as any seen in a football match. After two minutes George Best sparked the United revival when he latched on to a headed pass from Brian Kidd. Best whipped past his marker, Cruz, and then jinked his way around 'keeper Henrique to slip the ball into the back of the net.

In the third minute Kidd (celebrating his 19th birthday) headed United's third goal. And finally Bobby Charlton rattled home their fourth.

At last Manchester United were club champions of Europe. It had been a long journey, begun twelve years earlier, and one tinged with heartbreak and tragedy. At last Matt Busby's dream had come true.

In June 1968 the Queen honoured Busby with a knighthood, to add to the CBE he had been awarded in 1958.

The European Cup Final 1968 Manchester United v Benfica. Opposite page: *Bobby Charlton, scorer of two goals, takes on the Benfica defence.* Below: *Brian Kidd celebrates his goal and* above: *The United players parade the cup.*

THE RED DEVILS PROFILE

GEORGE BEST

George Best was first spotted as a youth by Bob Bishop, United's scout in Northern Ireland. "I think I've found a genius," Bishop reported to Matt Busby. And so the frail 15 year-old was brought over to Old Trafford from his native Belfast. But he was so homesick that he went home straight away! Thankfully Matt Busby was able to persuade him to return.

Best made his United debut in September 1963, in a 1-0 home victory over West Bromwich Albion. He made 17 League appearances that season and made his mark with players and fans alike, as a star in the making.

In the championship winning season of 1964-65 he was virtually ever-present (41 League games) and the scorer of 10 goals. By 1966-67 - United's next title winning season - George Best was a superstar, hailed as one of the best players in the world. Bob Bishop's prediction proved correct - George Best was a genius.

To see Best open up his box-of-tricks was a football fan's delight. With perfect balance, supreme skill and an underlying strength, he could beat one, two, even three or four defenders with apparent ease.

Best was the star of United's European Cup Final triumph against Benfica in 1968 - scoring the first goal in extra time and inspiring the team to a 4-1 win. 1968 also saw him voted Footballer of the Year in England and European Footballer of the Year. He was capped 37 times by Northern Ireland.

In 1974, due to private problems and pressures outside the game, George Best left Manchester United. He later played for Stockport County, Fulham, Cork Celtic, Hibernian, Motherwell and Bournemouth - and he enjoyed two spells in the North American Soccer League.

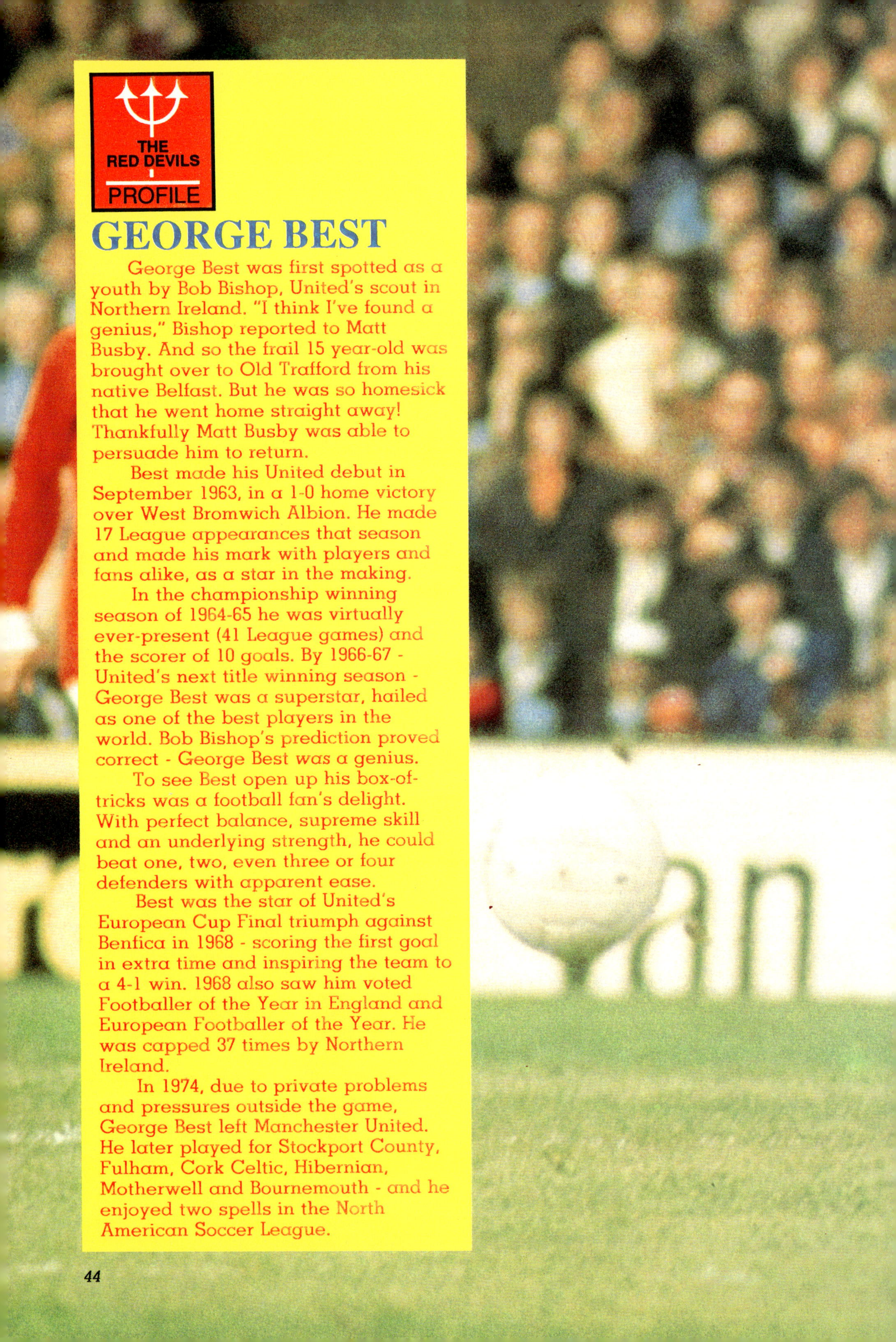

ALEX FERGUSON

THE
RED DEVILS
GUILIANO MAIORANA
SHARP

CHAPTER 12
CHANGES

The 1968-69 season saw United floundering a little in the League - they finished in 11th position. They also reached the semi-finals of the European Cup, but lost to AC Milan, the eventual winners of the trophy.

Sir Matt Busby announced his resignation in January 1969, after 24 years in the manager's chair at Old Trafford. His successor was Wilf McGuinness, a former 'Busby Babe' of the late '50's whose playing career had been cut short by injury. He took over the reins in June.

Although they reached the semi-finals of the FA Cup and the League Cup in 1969-70, United were not in true contention for the League title that season, and finished eighth.

The next season began badly. By Christmas 1970, United were dangerously close to the relegation zone and McGuinness found himself back behind the scenes, as coach to the reserves. The man to step into the breach was none other than Sir Matt Busby himself - a temporary measure while the search for a new manager was made.

In his customary manner Busby was able to raise morale, and this helped to improve the team's League standing so that they finished in a respectable 8th position.

The next manager, Frank O'Farrell, took over in July 1971. At first it seemed as if he was the miracle worker every United fan had hoped for. The team began the 1971-72 season in brilliant style - particularly George Best who was at the top of his form, scoring hat tricks against West Ham and Southampton. By Christmas, United were five points ahead in the Championship race.

Inexplicably the New Year saw a dramatic change - with no less than seven defeats in a row, and a terrible sinking feeling as the '*Red Devils*' toppled down the table.

O'Farrell acted quickly by paying out £125,000 for the services of top defender Martin Buchan from Aberdeen and £200,000 for winger Ian Storey-Moore from Nottingham Forest.

Buchan's steadying effect soon became apparent as United's form returned and they managed to finish in 8th position for the third year in succession.

1972-73 began badly for United. They did not record a win until the tenth game. In fact, they won just 12 League games all season and finished in 18th position.

Sadly, that season also saw the beginning of the end for George Best. Disciplinary problems and

Captain Martin Buchan and goalkeeper Alex Stepney doing a lap of honour with the Second Division Championship Trophy.

a certain disenchantment with the game had led to Best announcing his premature retirement from the game at the age of 26 (although he did play 12 games for United in the following season). Bobby Charlton also retired after serving United loyally for 17 seasons.

Frank O'Farrell went too. He was replaced by the flamboyant Tommy Docherty. "This is the greatest club in the world, and I am proud to be part of it ... I want to get the club back on its feet. We've got to get down to winning some games. We seem to have forgotten how to do that, " so said Docherty on his arrival at Old Trafford.

The 'Doc' then set about recruiting a 'Tartan Army' to strengthen United. He bought George Graham from Arsenal for £120,000, Alex Forsythe from Partick Thistle for £100,000 and Lou Macari for £200,000 from Celtic. In addition, he signed Jim Holton, Stewart Houston and Jim McCalliog - all in a massive rebuilding effort. Docherty also allowed Denis Law to leave Old Trafford on a free transfer to Manchester City.

But all these measures were to no avail - United finished the 1973-74 season just one place off the bottom of Division One. In the vital relegation issue match against Manchester City, it was, ironically, Denis Law's back heeled goal for City which effectively sealed United's fall into Division Two. On the last occasion when United had found themselves in the doldrums of the Second Division - 1937-38 - they had bounced right back again. Now they had to try and repeat that feat.

In the event, Manchester United dominated Division Two in 1974-75 and were top of the table throughout the season. They won the Second Division Championship with 61 points, ahead of Aston Villa and Norwich City.

Back in the First Division United put in some sterling work to finish 1975-76 in third position. That season also saw them making their sixth FA Cup Final appearance, against Lawrie McMenemy's Southampton. The match produced a famous 1-0 victory for *The Saints*, who were then a Second Division side.

Above: *Tommy Docherty who, on becoming United's manager, set about rebuilding the team with players such as Lou Macari* (below right). Below left: *Martin Buchan was a £125,000 buy from Aberdeen.* Below centre: *Ray Wilkins came to Old Trafford in August 1979.*

Twelve months later United were Wembley bound again - this time to meet Liverpool in the 1976-77 FA Cup Final. Liverpool were fighting for the 'double', having already secured the League Championship.

At half time the teams went into the tunnel without a goal being scored. It had been a dour battle with Liverpool having a slight advantage. But there was a surprise in store.

Manchester United were a team transformed in the opening minutes of the second half. Jimmy Greenhoff placed a perfect pass to the feet of Stuart Pearson. Pearson's shot whipped along the ground and slipped under Ray Clemence's body to finish in the back of the Liverpool goalmouth. Two minutes later Jimmy Case equalised for Liverpool with a superbly taken goal. Three minutes after that an error in the Liverpool defence was pounced upon by Greenhoff who rattled in a shot which rebounded to Lou Macari. Macari quickly fired in another which looked to be going well wide. Then it struck Greenhoff on the chest and was deflected into the goal. United won 2-1 and Liverpool's 'double' dream had to be shelved for a few more years.

1977-78 saw United finish 10th in the League and out of the Cup in the fourth round at the hands of West Bromwich Albion, managed by Ron Atkinson. By then Tommy Docherty was no longer United's manager - he had been dismissed after certain revelations about his private life.

Docherty was replaced by Dave Sexton, formerly manager of Chelsea and QPR, a quiet, thoughtful man, in complete contrast to the flamboyant 'Doc'. Sexton signed the powerful striker Joe Jordan for £350,000 and Gordon

Action from the 1979 FA Cup Final, Arsenal v Manchester United which the Londoners won 3-2.

McQueen for £495,000, both from Leeds United.

But United under Sexton had to wait for another season before near-success returned to Old Trafford. 1978-79 saw the club finish 9th in Division One - but they were also at Wembley for their third FA Cup Final in four seasons.

This time the opponents were Arsenal. The Gunners were two up by half time with goals from Frank Stapleton and Brian Talbot, United seemed a lacklustre outfit who did not deserve to win the cup. At least, that's how it seemed - until five minutes from the final whistle.

At that point big Gordon McQueen put United back in the game with a lunging left foot shot which beat Jennings in the Arsenal goal. The reborn United then surged forward again and Sammy McIlroy slipped through *The Gunners'* defence to score the equaliser - with less than two minutes left to play.

Then, the United players, perhaps convinced that the game would now go to extra time, momentarily lost their concentration - just long enough to allow Arsenal's Liam Brady and Graham Rix to build up another attack. The resulting cross found Alan Sunderland, and he scored the winner. The game became known as 'the five minute final' and one of the most disappointing moments in the history of Manchester United.

Ray Wilkins was the next major star to join the Old Trafford outfit. He was bought by Dave Sexton from Chelsea for £825,000 in August 1979. Wilkins' skill and tenacity in midfield contributed to a more consistent performance in the League and United finished the 1979-80 season as runners-up to Liverpool.

Gordon McQueen(red shirt), a commanding centre-half for United in the late '70's early '80's.

THE RED DEVILS PROFILE

BRYAN ROBSON

Bryan Robson joined Manchester United in October 1981. The fee paid to his former club, West Bromwich Albion, was a phenomenal £1.5 million, then a British record. Yet, when Robson was a boy it seemed unlikely that he would ever reach the top in soccer, for although he was talented, he was considered too slightly built to make the grade.

West Brom took a chance on the 15 year-old Robson who then weighed a mere 7 st. and stood just 5'2" tall. The club put him on a special diet to fatten him up. Within five months he had grown 3 and a half inches and his weight had increased by two stone.

Now 'Robbo' is considered one of the best players of the '80's. His reading of a game has been likened to that of such greats as Bobby Moore and Franz Beckenbauer. Despite an injury ridden career Bryan Robson has proved an inspirational captain for both Manchester United and England.

CHAPTER 13
MODERN UTD

Dave Sexton lost his job as Manchester United's manager in April 1981. After much soul searching by the club - during which they considered the likes of Brian Clough, Lawrie McMenemy and reportedly Bobby Robson - Sexton was finally replaced by Ron Atkinson.

Atkinson signed Frank Stapleton from Arsenal to bolster the attack and John Gidman from Everton to strengthen the defence. His most important signing, however, was that of Bryan Robson who arrived at Old Trafford, together with Remi Moses, in a £2 million deal from West Bromwich Albion.

Also making his mark in Atkinson's first season was a 17 year-old from Northern Ireland, named Norman Whiteside, another player destined to become a great favourite at Old Trafford.

In 1982 Atkinson signed the Dutch star Arnold Muhren from Ipswich. Peter Beardsley came to Old Trafford too, but played just one game for United before moving on to Newcastle.

The 1981-82 season saw United sign its first sponsorship deal with *Sharp*, the Japanese electronics firm, who had a depot in Newton Heath almost on the same spot where United had been born over 100 years earlier!

United did well in 1982-83 reaching the final of the Milk Cup at Wembley, against Liverpool. This turned out to be a tough encounter with Kevin Moran and Gordon McQueen both injured in the match. Nevertheless United clung on to a 1-1 scoreline, taking the game to extra time. Ronnie Whelan settled the matter by scoring Liverpool's winner with a spectacular shot.

United finished third in the League that season - but they also made it to the FA Cup Final, against Brighton. Along the way they had polished off West Ham 2-0, Luton Town 2-0, Derby County 1-0, Everton 1-0 and Arsenal 2-1 - none of these games had needed a replay. But the Cup Final did!

Brighton managed to surprise everyone by holding United 2-2 after

Above left and right: *Ray Wilkins scores a superb goal in the 1983 FA Cup Final against Brighton* and below left: *He celebrates his achievement.* Below right: *Arnold Muhren scores United's fourth goal from the penalty spot in the replay of the 1983 Cup Final.* Opposite page: *Norman Whiteside salutes the fans after scoring the only goal to defeat Everton in the 1985 FA Cup Final.*

extra time. Indeed Mick Robinson almost snatched victory for the 'Seagulls' in the dying minutes of the game. Only a brave dive by Gary Bailey at Robinson's feet was enough to save the day.

It was a different story in the replay at Wembley five days later. This time United ran riot over the luckless Brighton. Goals by Robson and Whiteside, inside a two minute spell in the first half, effectively put the game beyond Brighton's reach. Robson added a third just before half time. In the second half Muhren cracked in a fourth from the penalty spot. The 4-0 margin was the biggest win in an FA Cup Final at Wembley.

Two years later (1985) Manchester United were back at Wembley again, for their tenth FA Cup Final. Opponents Everton had already won the League Championship with 90 points. Like Liverpool eight years earlier, they were hoping to do the 'double' at United's expense.

The game was far from the classic it had promised to be and was marred by the sending-off of United's Kevin Moran for a questionable tackle on Peter Reid in the 78th minute. Moran and his team-mates protested his innocence, but to no avail. Referee Willis was adamant and Moran became the first player ever to be sent-off during an FA Cup Final.

Now United were spurred into action and the game came alive. After 90 minutes, however, the scoreline remained at 0-0 and the game went into extra time.

Ten minutes from the final whistle Norman Whiteside scored the winner with a fine, curling shot which beat Southall in the Everton goal.

The unfortunate Moran was refused a medal at the end of the match. However, he was presented with it a few weeks later after protests from the public, the press and on tv had proved that his tackle on Reid had not been as harsh as Mr Willis had at first thought.

Ron Atkinson continued as United's manager until November 1986, when he was relieved of his duties following a run of poor results. He was succeeded by Alex Ferguson, formerly manger of Aberdeen.

The second half of the '80's has seen Manchester United constantly challenging for top honours, in the best traditions of the club. But so far further success has eluded them.

The best season of recent years was 1987-88 when United finished as League runners-up to Liverpool. But so effective were Liverpool's performances that they tended to overshadow all other clubs, and United's achievement went largely unnoticed.

By 1988-89 Alex Ferguson had a strong-looking team of contenders led by skipper Bryan Robson. Goalkeeper Jim Leighton had been signed for £750,000 from Aberdeen; Mal Donaghy had been snapped up from Luton Town; Steve Bruce from Norwich City.

Centre-forward Brian McClair had been top scorer in 1987-88 and was the first United player since George Best to break the 20 goals barrier.

Lee Martin

The 1988-89 season also saw the return to Old Trafford of the Welsh International, Mark Hughes - via Barcelona and Bayern Munich. The homecoming did Mark a power of good and he was soon knocking in some spectacular goals.

There were high hopes at Old Trafford that United would once again be a footballing force to be reckoned with and there was much speculation that the Championship would soon be on its way back to the famous club.

However, things didn't quite work out that way. Injuries to key players meant an indifferent start for United in their quest for honours. Manager Alex Ferguson resisted the temptation to plunder the transfer market preferring instead to 'blood' several youngsters. That policy seemed to be paying off as all of a sudden memories of the Busby Babes came flooding back when the gentlemen of the Press coined a new

Guiliano Maiorana

term - 'Fergie's Fledglings'. These players included the 'Magnificent Seven ; Lee Sharpe, Lee Martin, Russell Beardsmore, Deinoil Graham, David Wilson, Mark Robins and Tony Gill. Their enthusiasm, and not inconsiderable skill, took United on an impressive unbeaten run which began on New Year's Day at Old Trafford when United thrashed Liverpool 3-1. Suddenly the League Championship began to look a possibility. Cup glory, too, was on the cards as United eased their way into the quarter-finals.

But things came to a dramatic, and somewhat controversial, end in that direction when, trailing 0-1 against Nottingham Forest, the referee ruled

Lee Sharpe

that a Brian McClair shot hadn't fully crossed the line. Television evidence later suggested that the 'goal' was good, but the referee's decision is always final, and United were out of the Cup.

Their exit from this competition also signalled a return to some mediocre League performances and United could only watch as Liverpool and Arsenal battled it out for the Championship.

But the future does look bright for United and if those 'fledglings' can come of age, then surely it will only be a matter of time before that elusive First Division Championship trophy is back at Old Trafford.

Russell Beardsmore

ROLL of HONOUR

League Champions:
1907-08, 1910-11, 1951-52, 1955-56, 1956-57, 1964-65, 1966-67.

League Runners-up:
1946-47, 1947-48, 1948-49, 1950-51, 1958-59, 1963-64, 1967-68, 1979-80, 1987-88.

Division Two Champions:
1935-36, 1974-75.

Division Two Runners-up:
1896-97, 1905-06, 1924-25, 1937-38.

F.A. Cup Winners:
1909, 1948, 1963, 1977, 1983, 1985.

F.A. Cup Runners-up:
1957, 1958, 1976, 1979.

Milk Cup Winners:
1982-83.

European Cup Winners:
1967-68.

Wilf McGuinness with the United team.

Alex Ferguson

MANCHESTER UNITED MANAGERS

A.H. Albut
1890-1900
James West
1900-1903
Earnest Mangnall
1903-1912
T.J. Wallworth
1912
J.J. Bentley
1912-1916
J.R. Robson
1916-1921
John A. Chapman
1921-1926
Clarence G. Hilditch
1926-1927
Herbert S. Bamlett
1927-1931
A.Scott Duncan
1932-1937
Sir Matt Busby
1945-1969
(Jimmy Murphy)
1958
Wilf McGuinness
1969-70
Frank O' Farrell
1971-1972
Tommy Docherty
1972-1977
Dave Sexton
1977-1981
Ron Atkinson
1981-1986
Alex Ferguson
1986-

Dave Sexton

Ron Atkinson

Frank O'Farrell

SHARP
SHARP
MANCHESTER UNITED F.C.